Steal It Back

Sandra Simonds

Distributed by University Press of New England
Hanover and London

Saturnalia Books
105 Woodside Rd.
Ardmore, PA 19003
info@saturnaliabooks.com

ISBN: 978-0-9915454-9-0
Library of Congress Control Number: 2015945808

Book Design by Saturnalia Books
Printing by Westcan Printing Group, Canada

Cover Art: Saturnalia Books, Inc.

Distributed by:
University Press of New England
1 Court Street
Lebanon, NH 03766
800-421-1561

Thanks to the editors of the *American Poetry Review*, *Granta*, *Lana Turner: A Journal of Poetry and Opinion*, *Ploughshares*, *Columbia Poetry Review*, *The Awl*, *Colorado Review*, *Poets.org*, *Boston Review*, *Fence*, *OMG*, *Catch-up*, and *Pinwheel* where these poems first appeared.

"I Grade Online Humanities Tests" was in included in the *Best American Poetry 2014* edited by Terrance Hayes and "Similitude at Versailles" was included in the *Best American Poetry 2015* edited by Sherman Alexie.

Some lines in "The Lake Ella Variations" are riffs on poems by Brian Ang and Carol Snow. Much gratitude to them both.

Contents

Alice in America

Alice better drive her wet cunt faster than
Western Union Oklahoma horse hooves
Out into the night's capital-letters
Alice better become a worse debtor
Fail better? Never! Alice better fail worse
Than the open letter Empire of letters
One better for the American settler
Last stop on the chain-letter

This psychometric Republic
Houses astronomic debtors
With geometric heads and aches
Get well Never get better Their optometrists
Housed in glass malls Their glasses
Concave Alice moves in convex debit card
Transactions Alice holding wet contracts
Is not convinced Alice with ripped contact lenses
Her pupils ripe Her flesh always object
Her asymmetric breasts toujours touched by men in charge

Skinned-knee Alice in a desert
Crosswind the woodwinds played on
Alice as drowned doll eyes and antique boots
When as a child she read the ship sunk
She felt the joy of wind-leapt trees
Burn everything Sink everything please
All eyes on the thick-skinned
Stockbrokers' heaven a whirlwind

Of electronic devices the plane
In headwinds pressed on the continent
Bloody-minded the way women
Who are pressed into suburbs
Collapse the white supremacist minds
Of violent men who create
Money and ideas and dominance

Collision of passengers and jet fuel
A field of vision no less Parisian
Than communizing cell-division
Alice looks up each catastrophe
In her rhyming dictionary like a dying breed
Of Dionysian woman Like a convulsing town
Of complex strollers and baby cries and pesticides
From here on out, Alice, you must take sides
With your long-division

Autumn in Allah or Guatemala
In Golem Salem Gaza
Quebec in Caracas Dallas
In Oz In Hell there are fifteen synonyms for
Sex but only one word for the police force
There's Alice climbing on top of a body
To forget all these wars and bullets
There's Alice with Mutual Fund
Waldorf salads and alcohol
To ward off the inevitable toward

Alice,
My tome has come and yours will
Drone my time bomb My dollface My mask
Like a training drill or fire alarm or police baton
My passenger jet drones on the Black Dahlia's
Severed head like a mirror that says
This is all women Cut in half in
Fourths in eights
With the magician's wand
Alice, bombshell, babe, take my language
My genitalia and make
your bombed out bake sale
Break and rage glass poetry
Palaces into tatterdemalion

Oh Alice
Hold your dura mater close to
Your body of hot water
Make water like a squatter
Make gray water
Make red water
Make tonic water
Make whatever is berserk better
An iceberg or Gettysburg Make all your ideas
Address me

Occupying

They were building an askance Calvin They were asking They went on a
hunt They were in the Netherlands They were wearing ice cubes They
were a sphere of influence They were building a Catholic schoolgirl
They were split like Germans They were split like dogs They were in a
psalm They were in an amen sort of way They were easy They were not
They were easy They were not easy They were at ease They were
walking to the drugstore They had diarrhea They were uncomfortable
They were building a Catholic schoolgirl They were aggravated They
were not They were world weary aristocrats They were improvising They
were a congregation They were distracted from the role of worship They
were afraid of the West Nile virus They were us They were important
and American You are incredible! They were simple songs They were
antiphonal They were simple Catholic schoolchildren They were a choir
They were testing the waters They were building a Catholic schoolgirl
They were adverse They were trapping onions They were responsorial
They were geniuses! They were following the leader They were split like
dogs They were leaders themselves They were listening to one version of
the hallelujah They knew about the soloist They were singing the next
verse They knew about your church They were without a leader They
were interesting kings They did not recognize the song They knew the
old 100th They were a doxology They were reformed They were sitting
They were theologically pumped They retracted their statements They
were traditional They were not They were conventional They were not
They were all pretty They knew this They were much more political
They were divorced They were reading about Henry the 8th They were

rude They were not They did not want to listen to the king They did They did not want to follow the leader They did They did not want to sing the songs They did They did not They did sometimes They did always They did often They did not They were the outgrowth of anthems Were too! Were not! Did too! Did not! They were building a Catholic schoolgirl They were cats They were cats on stilts They ate onions They ate clams They were trained musicians They were reading They were large and electronic They were like grandmother's cookies They were eating BBQ pork They were vegans They ate beef They were hypocrites They told us we must take sides They were men They were enormous They were not They were mindful They cleaned banks at night They reflected the structure of the world They were timed They blew the trumpet in the new moon They refused They collected trash They collected toys They collected land They accumulate land They landed They have cut the land with time They have cut the milk with beef They have cut the beef with horns They have cut the horns with gods They have cut the gods with toys They have cut the toys with Catholic schoolgirls They have cut the Catholic schoolgirls with trumpets They have cut the trumpets with the leader They have cut the leader with land They have cut the land with time Your poems are immature and buzzing Your poems are immaculate And lewd Your poems are buzzing Your poem is waspy Your poems are as immature as they are cunning They are bougie They are biting They are like pieces of cake They are extreme They are elemental They are losing They are too long They bore me to death They are losers They are winners They are round They are soft They are longing They are important They are accumulating They are wealthy They are satanic They are round They are going on and on about nothing Your poems are truly special They are kindergarteners They are rejects They are rejecting They are bears They are timetables They are huge They are soft They are rejects They remember being published They explain They are the ultimate They were created at work They were working They were on their own time They were timed They were confused They were misinformed They missed you They loved you but whatever They were the opposite of something They had no idea They were confused They were boring They went on and on They were derivative They were crafty They were simple They were announcements They were long They did not stop You are incredible! They are magnificent They do not stop They are marginal They are cunning They went on and on They were repetitive They cared about your feelings They were rejecting you They were cups They were plates They were at dinner They were diarrhea They were cunning They disagreed They did not stop They remembered They were historic They were calm They were annoying They were nice You are so nice I want to kiss you You are incredible! They had no ethics They were rewinding They were so boring They climbed a mountain They were losers They were incredible! They went on and on They were passing the time They existed They existed to pass the time They passed out Their lines were not long enough Their lines were too short Their lines were historic Their lines were liars They died They were derivative They were expanding They were expunged They didn't understand They were incredible! They understood They went on and on They were unknowing They tended to be philosophical They tended to be sexy They tended to one another They had a tendency They tended to lambs They tended to bears They tended to their own needs They put themselves first They put themselves above everyone else They were arrogant They were conceited They were deceived They were nice They were unethical They were nice They were building a factory They were bears They were people They were men and women They were bears They were nice They tended to gardens They tended to make love They tended to be sexless They tended to make love on Fridays They tended to be sexless They were criminally insane! They were incredible! They went on and on They were givers They were more givers than takers Sometimes you tend to give Sometimes you tend to be a giver Sometimes you make love on Fridays You say this is derivative You say this is exponential You say this is boring You say this is mathematical You say I am using the Fibonacci sequence You say I am right You say I am conservative You say I am a loner You say I am derivative You say you make love on Fridays You say you are sexless She was so nice that it was extremely annoying She was nice and needy and nice She made you a carrot cake because she was so nice She was so nice and careful I am nice Okay, I am not She was interested in being nice She was nice Alice, are you nice? Maybe not She was flavored nice She was nice We was nice We was flavored nicely We was nice she was Were she nice? Was she never ever nice? Nice she was? Was she nice? We was nice? Nice Nicer Nicer and nicer Nicer still Nice Nice Lice are not nice Lice are lice Lice are not nice Not nice! Not nice Not Nice Not France Supposedly not Supposedly opposed The opposite The opposed Supposedly the opposite You are spectacular! You are formal and spectacular! Go for her For her? Fourier? Don't splash the water, friend The truth is that this poem was written using the Fibonacci Sequence That is a fib That is a bib That is a lobster That is Maine That is a man That is noise That is not That is not happening Oh god this is not happening There is our toddler There is our town I am nice This poem was written using the Fibonacci Sequence In that sense it is confessional I have heard many noises today Because I am typing That is a fib You are a fat liar and I am hateful So there I want to make a long, happy poem cry I am poking a stick in the torso of my long happy poem It will not cry Oh you think that this is so terrible? Well you try to write a better one, friend Well, you're right On target Right on On the right there lived a family It's gone Question: Alice, how can you write poems so inconsequential? Answer: Because I am self-conscious and nervous And trembling I love you so much you make me nervous That is not true No one makes me nervous because I am not a child I am chilling out It is Sunday It is Monday and I am still chilling out frying up a steak because I am nice This is beer This is a candle This is cupid This is nice Occupy Wall Street I made you cupcakes I made you bread I made you pumpkin pie I made you pumps I made you already I made you soon I made you love It was manmade I made you limp I made you Christ I miss you Christ I miss your nice manmade pumps I made you a factory I made you a factory I made you a factory I made you math I factored that I factored in everything I made you love It was manmade I made you limp I made you cave I made you most I manmade you most I handmade you most I handmade you mostly You are the most You are mostly You are worth the most You are worth the most of the most You are worth more You are more You're more and more fatiguing You're more fatiguing than a manmade man You are manly, Mom This one was mostly mannish He had the worst manners He was not spectacular He wasn't more We were trying We were perceiving We knew it immediately We knew it instantly We were eating We were fatigued I want to make you something only a wife can perceive I want to make you at least half of a nipple I want to make you at least half of a terrorist Their skies were outsourced They were half mad They were criminally negligent They were unaware I want to make you something only husbands can subtract like bread pudding These were the worst of times They were the worst Thus she happened upon a criminal The movement was made by power sources It was manmade They were bored to death They were boring I'm gift wrapping you half of a terrorist They used their sources I want to make you something only a wife can accumulate such as stocks Such as large bills Such as gold coins with mold on them Such as middle of the road poets with arrows who become extreme editors because they are in charge They delve deeply into sorting I want to make you something unreasonable that only a cousin can make Maybe a penis? They were accumulating sunsets They were going to die They knew not to know it They were men and that is why they remembered In this sense we are all Snow Vikings led by revolving pursuits They remembered They crossed it out I want to make you a laughing dog etc. They were asking for conventional poems I want to make you a conventional poem because I am so madly in love with you I would do anything Inside my conventional poem I will fall madly in love with my own whatever That is why I am reasonable and clear-headed like an ice sculpture Or Russian mobs eating large white steaks and telling secrets Your debt is my command The landlady owes me hundreds of dollars I've been overpaying her for months What she doesn't know is I'm building a house for her as a present Inside the house there will be a colorful tomb I will push her into this colorful tomb She doesn't know it yet I have so many tricks up my sleeve It's because I'm passive aggressive It's because I'm mean and violent Have you built a house with a colorful tomb at its center yet? You better get going, Sir I bet she is incredible! I bet she has been in the Rose Parade I bet she is incredible I bet she is learning I bet she has launched I bet she is clairvoyant I bet she is going on a long sea voyage I bet she is sea worthy I bet she is a vessel I bet she is a pirate I bet she is booty I bet she is a lot I bet she is on the telephone with you I bet she is a light brunette I bet she shaves her handprints off every night I bet she is incredible I bet she is going to be in the Rose Parade I bet she is a piece of gold I bet she is a treasure I bet she is incredible I bet she reads the New York Times silently I bet she is a lot of things I bet she is talking to you on the phone I bet she is brushing her hair I bet she is getting ready to go to yoga I bet she is incredible I bet she is a dancer I bet she is a lot of things I bet she is a reader I bet she is living with her elderly grandmother I bet she is a reader I bet she is a lot of things I bet she is incredible I bet she is an excellent typist I bet she is a lot of things I bet she has been to yoga today I bet she is noble I bet she speaks in hushed tones I bet she is a reader I bet she is a lot of things I bet she is incredible I bet she washes her hair a lot I bet she is holding a napkin I bet she is on the telephone I bet she is wearing pants I bet she is incredible I bet she is an incredible dancer I bet she is a lot of incredible things I bet she dances every night I bet she is a habitat I bet she polishes her nails sky blue I bet she is incredible I bet she speaks in riddles I bet she dances every night I bet she is incredible I bet she is in excellent condition I bet she is a dancer I bet she is a habitat I bet she owns a vehicle I bet she plays the flute I bet she dances every night I bet she has a good mechanic I bet she speaks in hushed tones I bet she is incredible I bet she makes muffins every night I bet she is incredible I bet she plays Monopoly The men were incompetent the women were dancers The men were incompetent The women were dancers I was freely espousing Doug The men were incompetent the women were dancers The men were incompetent the women were dancers I was freely espousing Dough The men were West of here the women were dancers The men were West of here the women were dancers I was freely espousing Doug The men were incompetent the women were dancers The men were incompetent the women were West of here I was freely espousing Dough

Glass Box

Today, *I think I can do this for you; I can make this box for you.*
　　I don khakis, the attire of the capitalist order.
The workers valued revelation and the gospel which means
　　　"good news" in Old English. Spilled Frappuccino on pants, cried,
"Oh no! Oh shit!" Then went down the soldiers of 33rd Punjabis of the British
　　　　Indian Army in khaki. I don the depicted details, the place where one
must implant some cultural memory. I am the third
　　　remove, unheard, unheeded so today I think I can make a glass
box for you, call it a cube. She said maybe you're in love
　　　　with your friend and I said I think I can do this for you.

I loved my friend but he loved someone else and I was very pregnant
      with another man's baby. The early martyrs watched the fires
set by the emperor's own agents. I was teaching
      the humanities again. My friend flew across the country
to visit his lover. I had to breastfeed, commute, buy gallon
      after gallon of milk. Read: this is just the diary of
an ordinary woman or "mom" living at the beginning of the 21st
      century. Dura-Europas, the small garrison town is really
a cubicle and you are typing a poem by Hopkins into the screen
      of the 21st century. When you feel hours, you mean years.

When my friend told me he was in love with someone else,
        my thoughts turned to Greco-Roman models
for inspiration. Also, the letdown
        of milk since the body is relentless. A troll on Twitter.
It was snowing on all the arches, on the atrium, the four
        chambers of a chicken's short-lived, factory-style heart.
The word "psalm" comes from the Greek word "to pluck
        a lyre." Maybe I can address you now. My husband
will be furious. Coward. Liar. A voice says, "Alice, why did
        you have another baby?" Exercise:
                reread the Ten Commandments

Could you suggest othercommandments
for inclusion in a modern version?
        Day went down. I wrote a love poem.
Then monotheism, belief in ethics, a covenant
        with God, and the bible's influence. I throw my bills,
unopened, into the recycling bin. The workers
        and the rise of universities. A friend tweeted endlessly
about boners and blowjobs. I bought her book.
        My husband said, "Alice, you really crossed
the wrong stripper." I felt the willpower to work slip.

The workers rushed into the gothic, the logic flowing
     like togas or lava. Some felt pain. Some felt Vesuvius.
  In *The Classroom of Henricus de Allemania*
at the University of Bologna, note the sleeping student
     at the lower right. Or does he weep? And why are his
fingers so ladylike? Is he really a woman? Does my
     friend know I want to hold him? Iceland approves
crowdsourced constitution. To explain, preach
     and dispute. We rearrange the mind in downward flight.

I have nothing to say to you.
I am a professor of some kind. I am a worker
of some kind. I am a mother of some kind.
I cannot see you. I am in debt. I can see you.
I am teaching a humanities course of some kind.
I want very badly to talk to you. I am in debt.
I am writing this for you but even the language
between us is a critique of these mental pyrotechnics.
I want my professorial chair! I want to dazzle you
with my technique! I am in debt.

I want to feel this longing for you but
     I am tired. Speak directly to the saint.
The dream Dante has of the eagle that swoops
     his little body from the Middle Ages and places it
in a burnt-out Best Buy. Ventura highway
     in the sunshine? Love inside the slow,
steady decline of the torqued empire, our abstractions
     intensified. To be totally oriented to "the next life" or
your eyes, so shaken when I saw you last.
 I thought you had written this poem
for me and, for a moment, felt very alive.

Turned off the pop song, its fumes everywhere.
On the way back from work bought milk, advised
    the dear self not to. I cannot act. The troll said I was old
and ugly. I laughed, thought about suicide. The week of visions
    rhymed with the work week. *Out of the outfits*
I wore on the red carpet, which one looks best?
    The workers walked into the City of Ladies to buy
bags of chestnuts and figs and it snowed.
    Shopkeepers, brides, prostitutes and peasant
women. My daughter is twelve pounds.
    This is the diary of a minor poet, a "mom" living

at the beginning of the 21st century.

    We—the workers and also my lover and my husband
as well as the man who rejected me, pulled back
        the curtain to find a wall. Then I wasn't so sure I was being
rejected. My lover texted me, "we need to talk,"
    I ran ten miles, cooked a vegetarian lasagna for my husband,
bought a pirate costume for my son.
    "The Indian Ocean is in Chicago," my son said.
If I don't correct him, I am a bad mom, bad sister,
    bad daughter, bad philosopher-king.

If Plath had had a Malibu beach house,
    she wouldn't have killed herself.
I will walk through the double doors of the century
    with all of the other workers. Red Rover,
Red Rover. We hold one another. I will lead
    them to victory. I am "a fighter."
And on the page representing February, the farm workers
    are warming themselves inside the cottage and the sheep
huddle together outside, but the thing the viewer most
    identifies with is the girl with steamy breath on the far right,
stumbling back through the snow
    and the frozen village in the far distance.

The Lake Ella Variations

Twin five-year-old girls throw balls of bread at the blue heron
       standing in the lake. Eye patch.
One woman wears a t-shirt that says "Property of Jesus," another
       wears one that says "Je t'adore."
Pink hamburger slime. Ammonia
     on the heaven sent, on where we went. Dis
  in
    fect
ant. War
    trope, Viet-
  nam-era helicopter, heliotrope. This is my token
of friendship. By the end
      of the poem, the heron will fall over on his side and die.

Why do you keep asking about the Indian burial ground of my childhood?
　　　Growing collards is easy—you toss some seeds
into the mound and… voilà! But here's the contaminant:
　　　This life that I hate more than anything.
"Here Pepito, have a 40." This apartment I despise
　　　more than life. And this lake: just the rambling on
　　　of an idiot. No one word contains
　　　inherent magic, Child Lake!
　　　Let me reiterate: You have my friendship,
but you can't take my word.

Some sort of giantess shot out of the lake with a yellow feather attached to her big toe.
Made me want to drink and listen to country music even though I'm pregnant.
Have I become this Southern and trashy? Can the paw of a tulip grow
    from the mouth of a dead dog? Oh little shepherd boy
of the valley, Oh little Christian checkout boy,

    Oh little green apron boy with the crappy gray eyes, let's watch
the sunrise over Georgia. Gave poetry book I hate five stars on Goodreads; I am
such a liar!
    What if I step on a syringe and get a disease?
Who's going to give me a lot of money so I can quit my day job and write this poetry?

A log truck rolled over on my commute
    and out spilled the lake trying to communicate by
dragging her circular pilgrims underwater.

What will impress the death cult? The beautiful, vacant
        death cult? What will impress the mirror-writing lump,
water's canto, her cinema,
        commerce's atomic center?
What will impress the cult of death, the cult
        of holes, of clothes, the cult of sharp elbows?
The empress of the lake is here, all ninety degree angles.
        (Hello, empress of the lake). She answers through her teeth of zeros, in geese.
To move five stones to the right is to enforce
        the odds. To pepper-spray a toddler in the springtime, Printemps Paris.

Today Rick Scott fired all the scientists at water management.
    Thanks a lot.
So much for documentary poetics. The ure ducts of erica o azy.
    Mom says these politicians just ruin people's lives
and at dinner Emily asks, "Where are all the journalists?"
    The lake is the center of some great wheel
of sheer rags. The centrifugal force pulls
    the molecules where they don't want to go.
One scientist packs up the stuff that's accumulated in her office.
    Coffee cups, data, cardboard box.
I want to name her pull— but how?
    Much more difficult than
        naming an unborn baby.

The song of the lake and the song of the human
    make
the electric chair.

The song of the hand and the syringe
    make
the bread maker.

The song of the wheat flour and sticker book
    make
the bed.

The song of the house and the tsunami
    make
the frogs.

The song of Alice and her walk
    make
the crucifix.

Maud gone. So Modernism.
   So Yeats, Laertes, skull, origin. Hulk Hogan?
Make no mistake, the lake mocks
   your own clay grin. A dandelion?
In the coffee shop one sorority girl compliments
   the whiteness of the other girl's teeth.
Psalm gone. (Problem solved). So Lady Gaga
   broken from her
egg of triumph.

Oh gigantic woman of the swept-away!
  On my doorstep this morning I found a red feather from your headdress,
the one made from a thousand caterpillar eyes, the one made with the spleens
    of a million snow geese.
In your body of waterwheels, in your scales
    and skins of figure eights, there were infinite crocodile clocks!
In your ten-thousand minnow fingers and toes carved from the tongue of turtles,
    the humongous orgasm-based human origin of falling stomach-pits
mixed counter-clockwise with debris suns
    and the moldy decibels of half-eaten hotdog buns.

Sam wrote today and said, "Remember when we had
  dinner in San Francisco with your friendly, stoner boyfriend?"
I had a friendly boyfriend? I have no mentor
  and I mentor no one.
Rain like scientific notation on the surface
  of the lake. A duckling ate a full-grown,
blue heron. The grassy kingdom celebrates
  the unlikely king by clinking wine glasses.

I fake the lake skin
  the fake mistake
the lake lament
  the skin the
lake I trim
  the lament I make
tackle the cage
  I cage the age
   of water
  liquid eyeliner

Beautiful, lovely, rich women live in New England.
　　Beautiful, lovely, rich women live in Massachusetts.
Always happy writing surreal poems even when they're doing porn.
They eat corn mostly and have long hair.
　When other women tell the beautiful, lovely, rich women of New England
to cut their hair, the beautiful, lovely, rich women
　　know it's a trap! They've read Darwin.
They have gone to the depths of the lake and pulled out their
　　consciousness. They put their breasts on backwards
and call themselves "spiritual."

How strange to be seven months pregnant and see
    the man you used to have sex with so glossy,
        confused and embalmed on the pages of SPIN
    magazine at a Barnes and Noble
in Tallahassee, Florida; his torso, Lilliputian, no
    bigger than the length of the metacarpal
of your third finger. I suppose I could
    get back on Facebook and try to friend
him and say "hey" but my interest
    is so shallow. The lake—it is shallow too.

Alice, girl with no belief
    system ties knots
into a rope
    while listening
to U2 on
    her headphones.

What? Well, not
    everyone in a poem
can have good taste.

Nostradamus says, "Bring to
    my table the flesh
of this lake's
    finest poet!"

"But, Nostradamus, she left town
    yesterday with a sign
taped to her
    chest that says

Give blood, get a
    chance to win

free iPad2 or Kindle
 Touch."

Alice,
 come home.

Your mother
 has made you
a bowl of soup.

Steal It Back

FRESCO, VILLA OF MYSTERIES

Give me a quiet garden, Horatio. One made of mouths, the skin
    of Dionysus and flowers spilling into the stone courtyard
  and let the courtyard not be made of the sun's lace
      for we must wait until the 16th century
for lace to make its appearance. Not of Venetian glass beads
    for no slave has yet been traded for glass. Rather let us
  build the openwork fabric of our garden
      on the fear in the body
of a simple virgin who approaches marriage and if the details
    of these frescoes are difficult to interpret, still, there can be
no argument as to their high quality.

ATRIUM, HOUSE OF THE SILVER WEDDING

Life must have been extremely comfortable at Pompeii.
  In the summer, the open plan of the house would help keep the interior cool.
My mother came rushing into the bedroom. I believed I was perishing
  along with everyone else. Tallahassee, invest in gold now.
      There was an eclipse. Tallahassee, we are waiting
    for you to invest in gold. All the charm and comforts of Pompeii
      pale in comparison to Imperial Rome. Tallahassee, get gold
shipped to your door. We specialize in buying old and broken
    gold and silver jewelry, as well as old US coins, foreign coins,
bullion from around the world, and sterling silver flatware and hollowware.

MODEL RECONSTRUCTION OF ANCIENT ROME

In the lower right is the Pantheon. We use a program called
  MODFLOW to model groundwater and drawdown
of the aquifer. The sun moves across the oculus
  as children dig holes in the garden.
  Today, I stole a few hours from work.
 The structure of the whole is a symbol of the world.
     The structure and I hate each other.
  Arches spring up. Do you want to go to Sephora?
Here I am. Sephora, gold mascara, symbol of stolen work.

HEAD OF THE COLOSSAL STATUE OF CONSTANTINE (I)

Simply being white is not indicative of power
   for some worked on peanut farms.
Yet, simply being white *is* indicative of power,
   for some worked on peanut farms.
The Roman Empire did not fall overnight.
  I spent the night making a presentation for
 faculty senate on our retirement package and our
promotion system. The soldiers felt no loyalty
   to the empire so their lives became abstractions.
They called the university a "family."
   At meetings, I could tell the workers wanted
to hold their babies and grandchildren. My daughter is
   13 pounds. Total collapse was prevented by
two emperors. Horatio, I live in the provinces.
   Horatio, I am minor. Therefore, all.

HEAD OF THE COLOSSAL STATUE OF CONSTANTINE (II)

At New Leaf Market, Ezekiel shouts,
  "I came out of mommy's uterus."
 I believe in the proper names of things.
   Let an intestine be called an intestine but don't
 let that forest be called Lake Ella unless
   Ezekiel is looking into the painting
and points to a dragon, a troll, an ogre.
   A woman approaches us and says
she taught her son the same thing
about names. "Where is he now?" I ask.
   "He is dead now," she says and leaves.

THE BIRTH OF THE OPERA

This man I loved, he did not love me
    and as fascinating as this may be—come to me,
        back to Tallahassee we buy
        silver, gold, melt down your
        engagement ring, wedding ring,
        anything, Tallahassee, spiral me, never me,
        opulent, see?—well, maybe
    he did love me after all. Nothing
  clear except a lack of metaphor,
    madrigal, musical jokes.
O the danger of the physical
  involving considerable breath control, porn.

JACOB BLESSING THE SONS OF JOSEPH (REMBRANDT)

It is 1656, the year of my financial collapse.
   When my husband and I were separated,
      my first thought was I cannot let anyone
fall into my debt. Asenath, Joseph's wife,
   should not fall into my debt. Nor Andrew.
Nor Mary. Nor Joseph. Not Ezekiel. Not
Charlotte. Not Alice. No one
   should fall. We walked by the US Mint
   which was etched into the coinage
of the Pacific. He never married
   Hendrickjs Stoffels and his unconventional
behavior alienated him still further
   from his contemporaries. At work, I place my
      index finger on the picture, the little family
   in a boat of heavy curtains, hair and paint.

HYACINTHE RIGAUD'S LOUIS XIV

Shut up, Louis, you are sooooooo not sixty-three
      in this painting!
    Plastic surgery and pop-tarts. Amazing!
Ermine-lined robes, mission creep, drones,
      Ann Romney let them eat—wrong Louis, Alice.
Wrong Louis!—skip
    ahead thirty pages, exchange the I and V,
      the object and subject, figure
and head, history and princess,
    Roman and iPhone—
Qu'ils mangent de la brioche—
    the God particle and stock market.

THE HALL OF MIRRORS

Sephora, this one's for my sagging face
        and the service worker who wants to sell me
pink hair mascara. She is poor; let her
    sell. This poem is for my debit
card. My daughter is 14 pounds.
    And it is also for the legislation
of my uterus. Sephora, don't say it
    in public. Don't say it on the floor.
        Don't be too political. Why don't you
        respond to my advances? Why such a cold,
uncaring bitch? My mother used to say
    I am so sick of picking
up after you. She'd chase us around
    the apartment with a hairbrush.

MARCHESA ELENA GRIMALDI, WIFE OF MARCHESE
NICOLA CATTANEO

This red umbrella points West
        but I will not hold it. Instead, I will hold a branch
and I will never turn around
        to see what I have done.

I Grade Online Humanities Tests

at McDonald's where there are no black people
and there's a multiple choice question
or white people about Don Quixote
or Asian or Indian people I don't want to be around
people I want to be here where there is
free wireless I do not want to sit at the Christian
coffee shop or the public
library No, I want religion to blow itself up
My sister converted to Catholicism
I do not want to sit at Starbucks
I like McDonald's coffee because it is cheap
and watery I like how it tastes
I like this table where the old man
is telling his old friend
about the baby black swans he would feed
corn to in Cairo, Georgia when he was a kid
No, Mark Twain did not write Don Quixote I'm going to
be here a while in this fucked up shit
You can get an old Crown Vic police car
In Cairo for $500 so I read
a poem by James Franco
in the literary magazine I brought with me
My mechanic wants to fuck me
and the poem isn't as bad

as people say he is bad One of his friends dies
in the poem He uses the word "cunt" I don't know
what to make of it I read it as "Cnut"
the medieval prince of Denmark who ascended and ascended
to become the king of England I bet some managers here could relate
to Cnut Send me a pic of your
cunt the mechanic says I miss you I say what do
you miss about me He says "your big tits"
Elliott Smith is mentioned in
the Franco poem and might or might not
be a "cowboy" Maybe Franco really
is bad after all The Crown Vic is
a vehicle the way the police always
say "vehicle" not "car" but the mechanic
always says "car" not "vehicle" because I teach
the police I know how they talk The mechanic
says Alice, stop speeding and do you want
to see a picture of my wife No Cervantes
did not write "Because I Could Not
Stop for Death" and I will be
sitting here all day in this fucked up shit god
dammit click click click I keep looking
at things like pictures of your husband
which makes me feel sick
and watery Now a young boy maybe 8 or 10
in a booth across from me
is telling his mama his daddy's new girlfriend is ugly
"She's ugly, mama" and trying to comfort her
Do you want to meet in the Home Depot
parking lot? I don't think this is a good

If I find you with him I'll kill him
and I'll kill you and no one will
know where your body But your husband
isn't ugly he is beautiful leaning over to look at himself
in pond water or leaning over
masculinity itself leaning over the family
he has made for himself and the pond
is male because he owns the pond
and the guns are male because he owns the guns
and what's happening is male because he owns the factors
that go into the car is male because he owns the police
and Home Depot is male because he owns and owns
and owns and all he can do is own
everything that will rot
like privacy or speech or porn or black swans
or my big tits which he misses
Fucking swans! A man decides to sit
next to me and he is frantically hitting
his Egg McMuffin on the table and then walks
outside and smokes a cigarette and returns
to his seat and starts hitting
his wrapped Egg McMuffin again
and then he sees my computer and asks
to check his Facebook so I let him
and then he wants to be friends on Facebook
and leaves his phone number on my page
and I "like" it and then in the background
the little boy's like "She's ugly, mama
She's so ugly mama" and the mom
is like "Is she? Is she ugly?" And I think the mom

is ugly even though I don't want her to be
and the other kids at the booth
are drinking milk and they are chubby
and eating fries and saying
"Yeah she's ugly
Yeah mama she's so ugly
You wouldn't want to meet her
because she's so ugly"

A Poem for Landlords

Today I paid my landlord
at the last possible minute
on the last possible day
of the month which is
on the 5th day of the month.
It is the 5th of November, 2012.

Poets hate their landlords.
This is an imperative. It has no grammar.
Maybe it has a crude grammar.
I am not writing the check until
the last possible minute
in my car because I have
so much hatred in my heart
for property and landlords
but not land or streams
since I love the Romantics
since I am also a romantic
when I am not practicing
stupid conceptual poetry
like going to TJ Maxx
and looking at my face.

I have been thinking
of the body of my three-year old

and how it is so new and unstable
and how I don't want him to ever feel
happy in this world.
I don't mean it like that.
I want him to feel joy
but not happy in the sense
that he feels content.
I want him to feel
contempt for landlords
the same way that I feel
contempt for landlords
and how I have hated them all
in exactly the same way
which is an abstract hatred
since it reaches into the future
as well as a concrete hatred
since it is right here
in my parked car as
I write this rent check
and how this hatred is sophisticated
in the manner of a Marxist
and how it is unsophisticated
like the juvenile delinquent
I will always be even when
I'm very old because
for whatever reason
that simply could not
be beaten out of me.

So back to this check
I don't want to write

and writing the numbers
of amounts of money
and my name in cursive
which is the last place
in the world in which I use cursive
and this is also the last place
where I write checks and how
if I don't do this
I would need
to get a money order
from now on
to pay the landlord
I despise who are all
exactly the same
and whose threats are
all exactly the same.

I do not want to feel this hatred.
My daughter is twenty pounds.
I want to feel joy and I want
my little infant to feel joy
and I don't want her
to grow to be happy.
I don't mean it like that.
I want her to feel joy
when she walks in a forest
or by a river looking at birds.
If she feels one day
a "seething contempt,"
I will be proud of her for I shall know
she is my daughter.

I know that I should be happy
for my children
if they are happy.
Oh don't become tax collectors!

I am writing this so quickly.
Soon Craig will be home
and I will need to breastfeed
and cook dinner.
I am writing this so fast.
I will not be able to look
back at it but just now
I am looking back at it since I made
dinner and cleaned the house
and I am also revising it
and thinking about how
my anger has subsided
because at dinner Ezekiel
told me he kissed
his friend on the cheek at school
and he says it is "okay to hug
a friend but we
don't kiss friends at school."

I will post this on my blog
immediately.

It is Nov 5th, 2012.

Journey of Marie De Medici

Paintings of this scale require the help of assistants.
  We are the sum total
of our social relations.
 Rubens is not an intimate painter but his pictures
convey the restless
      energy of his life.
 I am going on a five mile run this morning before
I take my children to the museum. It is Sunday,
October 28, 2012. God will enter
   the picture, but only in the places
where the painter didn't intend—on the white knee
  of the defiant horse who has no
    desire to go into battle, in the pupil of a cloud,
     in the splash of the king's chamber pot
as the servant carries it out into
   a winter morning.

   Warhol had elves who helped him paint
     the words "Cheddar Cheese,"
"Onion" and "Vegetable Bean"
onto his canvases. I run past the closed
    down Safeway, see three kittens under
a palm tree, imagine the kittens and palm
   as the up / down digits
of the stock market. Wait! These things
are not things. They are not
   information! They are not
money! They are three kittens
   and a tree. My daughter
     is eighteen pounds.

Today the troll on Twitter calls my friend
a "fat hog." Warhol's cans are elegant,
        painterly even. I, too, need a community
              of poets, or at least
        a few who will read my work
        and confirm that I should keep writing
and when I think of you, I tell myself
        to try to be a good person
        as if that's all that matters
and then desire. I miss you.
        "It's all projection," my friend said
when I told him about the troll.

Why did you abandon me inside
        the humanities? I clipped coupons
        to no avail. I trained for a half marathon.
        Nothing. Look at the queen on horseback
at the Battle of Ponts-de-Cé; regard the fame
        and glory that flutter around her head.
        The factory and the workshop.
                The dying, the dead.
Follow me on Twitter, and then follow
        the nightlife fixture, the "party girl,"
        in the role of vixen. All of this
        accidental literature. When Warhol
was told Edie Sedgwick had died
        his response, cold and calculating
        as that king's piss, was
                "Edie who?"

The Abstract Humanities

1.

On August 14th, 1971, when they arrest Jason Smith on Rose St.,
   his neighbors don't know he's a subject
 in the Stanford Prison experiment, and Jason himself
doesn't know that within 36 hours of dunking his head
  into that fake cop car, that he will have a mental breakdown
even though he keeps telling himself "this isn't real."
    Daumier's "The Third-Class Carriage." This isn't real.
      Turnitin.com. This isn't real.
    Bingham's "Fur Traders Descending the Missouri."
  This isn't real. In solitary confinement he thinks
of his grandmother, Pearl, the only woman who
has loved him unconditionally
    and finally recognizes Todd,
the guard, as the student who sits in the row
 in front of him in Biochemistry. Our quiz will be on
    Ludwig van Beethoven's "Pathétique,"
    Charles Darwin's theory of natural selection.
      On destiny, 35.
      On disillusionment, 543.
    On empires, 96. On imperialism, 467.

2.

Do you know how many of Karl Marx's
     children starved to death?
  Yes, but he kept a maid.
      Did you know two of his daughters
               committed suicide?
      Do you know the difference between pity
  and compassion? My daughter is 30
pounds. This isn't real.
      Do you know the difference
         between compassion and empathy?
               I am bleeding.
   It is easy to be empathic and lack compassion
      but sometimes a person is compassionate and lacks
  empathy. The limit case being a saint or
               martyr. To write the most tender
         poem for Karl Marx,
      which includes the Torah or rather the light
  of the Hebrew alphabet which casts
               its glyphs on one
  of Rembrandt's wide-eyed, apple cider walls.

3.

Do not write "luminous glyphs" for it is
     overly Romanic. Do not write
  a love poem to Karl Marx
      for you might lose your job.
         Do not talk about compassion, for this is not

a temple. Do not use the word "tender"
    for this is art and art must be
cold like money or fish. Do not
    say you're a Jew
    for you never know who is reading.
Do not place the word "money" next to the word
"Jew" for people will think that all
    you care about is money.
        On patronage, 310. On pride, 59.
      On reform, 331. I am shaking.
      On scientific truth, 387.
               I'm scared I will die.

4.

      It has been fifteen years since my mother
    tried to kill herself. There is no way
      into the humanities. In the experiment, Todd
    beats Jason. You can only follow
me so far, but when we get to the river, Horatio,
    you will not be able to cross through my
particular hourglass: Ubermensch, 468.
    Ulysses, 533. *Un Chien Andalou*, 552.
          It is hard to believe that I found her.
It is hard to believe that I lived in that apartment
    with my mother and sister.
It is hard to believe that I was at her side
    in the hospital. The bourgeoisie
    are so self-destructive!
That's the real secret of the *Communist*

Manifesto. On the phone she says,
"Why do you think about things
    that happened so long ago?"

5.

        Horatio also says, let the past
            be the past, doomsday, doomsday.
                Zeno, 343. Zeno, 2.
                        I'm scared and I'm bleeding.
                Zen philosophy, 596.
        Let the peasant in this painting reap
what she sows, and if nothing comes
of nothing, Zero, Zero, let the mother
        of the third-class carriage's weeping
hands over woven basket, infant
        to the nipple, rest unseen.

Similitude at Versailles

Welcome to Humanities 203!
Here you will find the mysterious
death of the honeybee, the Byzantine emperor,
Justinian, who made church and state
a seamless whole. Quiz tomorrow.
When someone dies, you buy their relatives flowers.
1-800-FLOWERS. As a result
your driving privilege will be suspended
indefinitely on 11/13/2012.
Where's mommy?
I said I was trying to write this poem
for the day, do you mind?
The Real Ghostbusters will return
after these messages. The trap's ready.
I can get a girlfriend anytime I want.

On the toddler bed, wrapped in the felt
blanket with monkeys printed all over it,
their prehensile tails curled—
I promise guys, I'll never let myself
get carried away by women again. I want pancakes.
Hey Alice, I think Charlotte might be hungry.
I'll be there in a second.
Okay, I'll just feed her now.
Charlotte is 38 pounds.

—what could pass as love inside capital?
Maybe just these records, the real.
   At the Halloween festival, my friend dressed
   her child as one of the 1%. Ezekiel
      was a pirate. Her little girl threw
         fake bills into the air. She danced
in her suit and mustache. Thought—
   it will only ever snow $ in Florida

and you seemed more like the bas relief,
the minor key, some detail about Louis XIV's
      weak blood I always forget to teach,
      and for a moment I had become
   the anarchy of the sea—you know how the waves
are always pounding out some polyphony
      in saltwater, algae and fish
         their subjects cannot understand.

Poem With Lines From Pierre Reverdy

Maybe the world will not be saved.
It will not be saved. Its commerce, its
every case moves into it's geology
and then that geology moves
into some great exit of slowing
clocks and the history of saved light.

Listen, I'm not crazy. I want you to save
something for me. If someone says
something false, I will tell that person
"you are false" because I am full
of exaggerations and energy
and also because sunlight scatters
across this lake and just one beam
is enough to make my body insane.

The world will not be saved by despair
so we should spend it all on joy, right?
I despair. Does he despair? The desperate
characters walk onto the stage.
The stage a lake the lake a self I staged
The lake the self I staged. They sing
off key like me. There is no
harmony but when the children clap their
little hands, well, neither is there simile.
I washed the dishes; I folded the laundry.
I wanted to walk around
this lake like an innocent.

Lake Eden

I walked to the lake. I passed the Hooters, Publix, McDonald's
where I sometimes use the internet to grade papers
        when my neighbor's internet is down. I passed the Wendy's,
and the Scottish Rites temple, whatever that is. When I got to the coffee shop,
    I ran into Vince and John and we talked for a moment
        and I thought I can't believe I'm drinking
more coffee really giving Balzac a run for his money.

        Then it began to rain, but I am not afraid of rain.
Then it came into my head that I am not a professional poet though
    we now are surrounded by professionals. I got very happy and it was
still raining but a light rain. I said to myself, "Alice, you are not
        a professional!" *Wait, what is a professional?*

    I always sense the total. I thought about my record player,
how all the music sounds like recordings of music
        and how this somehow gives me back a history, both personal
and abstract, since the form and the mechanism of the form
        are one. Never have I bought one article of clothing

        on the internet. Never have I taken a drug
I didn't understand. Never have I listened to the lake exchange
            place with the rain. So, Lake Eden,
        go ahead and read your Chinese philosophy if you think
            that is what will make you sane.

Eclogue

Waves of Russian bots on makeshift Cuban boats ask for my hand in skin-tone.
Grandiose invasion of spring Mongolians perestroika down the Asian steppe, disseminate
in floral digits and April crept. Khan's genes ringtone Sephora where I buy an eyeliner called
"Diva at Dawn." Was content. Maybe I drink so much coffee in the evening
because I drink so much vodka in the morning. In Luanda, it costs
sixteen dollars for an apple, in Abu Dhabi, an outdated source
eats horse. Mohawk sky in Dusseldorf does me good.
Glenn Beck in a dugout canoe in the hood. Lana Del Rey with American flag,
dick and bike. He looks up from his sandwich, says, "alright."
Hitler! Bieber! The gold map! Sea-torn yet flowery, like a liver overlaid
on the foamy bot, transplant, topographic pirate in sinkhole of insecticide and Sriracha.

Outside Orlando we ate kimchi, exchanged gelatinous-like substances, smoked pot
and when we left the shore, we were only the transport flesh of genetic material carrying records
into the forensic tide of the three-dimensional Gulf of Mexico.
Sensei, what is the point of making this report? Bros at the LA Air Force Base
gather round a piece of brie like Christmas carols. One asks me,
"Are you from Cleveland? I repeat, are you from Cleveland?"
I have no time for this. I've become too uppity with my risk.

Eclogue

State Department sponsored austauschülerins gravitating towards the innermost,
    syntactically-warped,
        clocks of Dresden. Straight-A schülerins, haughty and viral,
            dummy-like beauties, meant to reproduce
                war rooms, repeating the words
        "citoyen du (monde." Womb)
            with chunks of broken off Berlin Wall wrapped in
        old fashioned, cloth napkins—the trade routes blue-blooded varicose
                veins, slow and fat. Boom to the haute-
                    route Alp or deep south
        surveillance mechanism—all explosions need time—
to enact some backward, joyous revenge,
        to practice Jan took my countdown pen--(the half life
of neptunium=2.14 million years) "War ist.
        Du bist. Ich," seen through the parabolic sketch
            on the next page—notes
                on the electron microscope, ties orchid to
                    its pole with a dollar bill.

    Then Alice, the protagonist climbs the bust of Goethe, overlooking
        some subatomic skull-fractured wilderness,
            bombardment kissed ("you have
                no accent"), then bused back to our separate
                geographic hinges. I imagine
            something in the trees ticking like ovens
        accidentally left on, some genetically modified phrase or
            drone eyes ablaze, braids down to waist,
                yodeling like the age
                    reborn in its history of forgery.

I am Inside the Humanities and

                    if I step
                    too far out of it,
                         I'm dead. The figure
                    at the top left corner is Securitas.
              No rent! No work! No wages!
               No more! For those thinking
            of disturbing the peace, let
              the hanged man be your warning.
      In order to write this poem,
           I paid daycare $523
                    for the week. Make sure you premix
                the bottles, bring diapers. Make it worth
                         something, this time. Mayan
                    countdown clock to Mayan
      countdown clock, two bodies,
                in a bed wanting
              the water of the world to
      give them back a pyramid.

                    Also, the bronze head of Adam.
                         Also, the world of children,
                      their toys, the plastic imitation food—eggs,
                    miniature cereal boxes, deformed mirror
                    to the real. I could not keep working
                to make money for the people I despised,
                    nothing is right, but I couldn't afford
                    not to either. Late at night, Craig
                         said "I hate my job." The hydrologists
                    have to give permits to Gulf Oil

for more water or someone
will get fired. It was winter
in Florida, the path to all principles
of all inquiries led back to this
one statement, like a receipt
from Publix: I was teaching
the humanities again.

In the garden of the fallen
aristocrats, where no one sits
on the lawn, it is as if heaven is on
one side, hell, on the other,
and somehow I have slipped very far
into the abyss between the two,
an abyss that contains suns
the way black holes
do not give back the history
of light, the way a galaxy
turns like a clock
into the desperate desire
for water and these flowers—
what can I make of them?
They bloom like idiots,
live as thieves.

I get Craig's cryptic texts
from West Florida
    on my walk at Lake Ella: "No coffee.
    Nuclear power plant" and then he sends
        a picture of some industrial
            map of rust.

O Apollinaire, eau-de-vie,
    in this garden, which is a mockery
        of all gardens,
    in this Bed, Bath and Beyond
of the intimate, remember me.
        My daughter is 43 pounds.
    I know what is real
    and I know how to steal
        back what is mine.

Winners of the Saturnalia Books Poetry Prize:

Neighbors by Jay Nebel

Thieves in the Afterlife by Kendra DeColo

Lullaby (with Exit Sign) by Hadara Bar-Nadav

My Scarlet Ways by Tanya Larkin

The Little Office of the Immaculate Conception by Martha Silano

Personification by Margaret Ronda

To the Bone by Sebastian Agudelo

Famous Last Words by Catherine Pierce

Dummy Fire by Sarah Vap

Correspondence by Kathleen Graber

The Babies by Sabrina Orah Mark

Also Available from saturnalia books:

In Memory of Brilliance and Value by Michael Robins

Industry of Brief Distraction by Laurie Saurborn Young

That Our Eyes Be Rigged by Kristi Maxwell

Don't Go Back to Sleep by Timothy Liu

Reckless Lovely by Martha Silano

A spell of songs by Peter Jay Shippy

Each Chartered Street by Sebastian Agudelo

No Object by Natalie Shapero

Nowhere Fast by William Kulik

Arco Iris by Sarah Vap

The Girls of Peculiar by Catherine Pierce

Xing by Debora Kuan

Other Romes by Derek Mong

Faulkner's Rosary by Sarah Vap

Gurlesque: the new grrly, grotesque, burlesque poetics edited by Lara Glenum and Arielle Greenberg

Tsim Tsum by Sabrina Orah Mark

Hush Sessions by Kristi Maxwell

Days of Unwilling by Cal Bedient

Letters to Poets: Conversations about Poetics, Politics, and Community
edited by Jennifer Firestone and Dana Teen Lomax

Artist/Poet Collaboration Series:

Velleity's Shade by Star Black / Artwork by Bill Knott
Polytheogamy by Timothy Liu / Artwork by Greg Drasler
Midnights by Jane Miller / Artwork by Beverly Pepper
Stigmata Errata Etcetera by Bill Knott / Artwork by Star Black
Ing Grish by John Yau / Artwork by Thomas Nozkowski
Blackboards by Tomaz Salamun / Artwork by Metka Krasovec

Steal It Back was printed using the font Minister Book and Franklin Gothic.

www.saturnaliabooks.org